Making Jewelry
with Scrapbook Embellishments

KRISTIN DETRICK

NORTH LIGHT BOOKS

CINCINNATI, OHIO
www.artistsnetwork.com

10 09 08 07 06   5 4 3 2 1

Distributed in Canada by Fraser Direct
100 Armstrong Avenue
Georgetown, ON, Canada L7G 5S4
Tel: (905) 877-4411

Distributed in the U.K. and Europe by David & Charles
Brunel House, Newton Abbot, Devon, TQ12 4PU, England
Tel: (+44) 1626 323200, Fax: (+44) 1626 323319
Email: mail@davidandcharles.co.uk

Distributed in Australia by Capricorn Link
P.O. Box 704, S. Windsor, NSW 2756 Australia
Tel: (02) 4577-3555

Library of Congress Cataloging-in-Publication Data

Detrick, Kristin
  Making jewelry with scrapbook embellishments / Kristin Detrick.
     p. cm.
  Includes index.
  ISBN 1-58180-689-2 (alk. paper)
  1. Jewelry making. 2. Scrapbooks--Equipment and supplies. I. Title.
  TT212.D46 2005
  745.594'2--dc22
                              2005011975

editor David Oeters

designer Leigh Ann Lentz

layout artist Jessica Schultz

production coordinator Robin Richie

photographers Christine Polomsky and Al Parrish

stylist Nora Martini

dedication

*I dedicate this book to
my husband, Doug, and
our wonderful daughter,
Elizabeth. Thank you
for your love and
your support, and for
your patience with my
sometimes time-intensive,
schedule-driven freelance
design career!*

about the author

Kristin Detrick is an independent freelance designer who has worked primarily for *Better Homes and Gardens,* Meredith Corporation.

Kristin's designs have appeared in numerous Meredith magazine publications, including *Creative Home, Simply Handmade, Craft For Kids, Creative Kids, Quick & Easy Christmas, Christmas Ideas, Countdown to Christmas* and *Holiday Celebrations.* Her designs have been featured in several Meredith books, including *Christmas from the Heart, Celebrate the Season, Easy Beading, Crafting with 4 Supplies, Crafts for Girls Only, Spider-Man Party Book* and *Easy Crafts to Make Together.* Kristin's designs have also appeared in *Christmas Together* by Brave Ink Press.

Kristin freelances as a prop buyer and photo assistant for Meredith photography sessions. She has over twenty years experience in art, primarily in clay, metals, painting, stained glass and three-dimensional art (mixed media). Kristin also has a two-year fine jeweler's apprenticeship.

METRIC CONVERSION CHART

to convert	to	multiply by
Inches	Centimeters	2.54
Centimeters	Inches	0.4
Feet	Centimeters	30.5
Centimeters	Feet	0.03
Yards	Meters	0.9
Meters	Yards	1.1
Sq. Inches	Sq. Centimeters	6.45
Sq. Centimeters	Sq. Inches	0.16
Sq. Feet	Sq. Meters	0.09
Sq. Meters	Sq. Feet	10.8
Sq. Yards	Sq. Meters	0.8
Sq. Meters	Sq. Yards	1.2
Pounds	Kilograms	0.45
Kilograms	Pounds	2.2
Ounces	Grams	28.4
Grams	Ounces	0.04

acknowledgments

I would like to thank Heidi Boyd for all her help, support and encouragement in making this book.

I would also like to acknowledge Linda Franklin of Memory Bound in Ankeny, Iowa. Linda, with her vast knowledge of scrapbooking, was of great help to me in creating this book.

table of contents

embellishments everywhere!
14

chapter 1

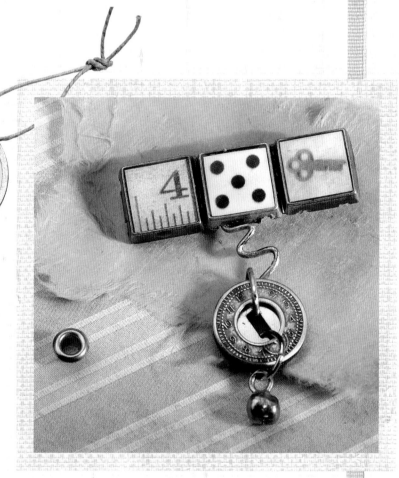

Create!

introduction

I first came across scrapbook embellishments when I worked as a greeting card freelance designer. Each time I visited a scrapbook store for material, I noticed more and more embellishments. The embellishments were so eye-catching and creative. The surge continued as large craft stores began to devote entire aisles to display scrapbook embellishments, specifically designed to decorate scrapbook pages, but useful for so much more. It didn't take long for me to begin using these embellishments in craft designs other than cards and scrapbooks. That's when I began making scrapbook jewelry.

If you walk into a scrapbook store and think *jewelry* instead of **scrapbooking**, you'll see what I mean. And once you have some background in basic tools and techniques, you'll see how easy it is to incorporate scrapbook embellishments into pieces of jewelry. You'll see the full potential of these fabulous products.

I'm still amazed by the embellishments filling the aisles every time I walk into Memory Bound or Heirlooms By Design, local scrapbook stores in my area. In this book, I have used recognizable scrapbook products by wonderful companies such as 7gypsies, American Traditional Designs, ARTchix Studio, EK Success, Making Memories, Nunn Design and Pebbles, Inc. I hope you will enjoy working with their products as much as I have.

In the following pages, I'll explain the basic tools you'll need to create your own jewelry. I'll also cover basic techniques and show you how to use glues, primers and varnishes, and how to manipulate metal surfaces—very important steps in converting some embellishments into jewelry elements. This knowledge and your own creativity will empower you to create many beautiful jewelry designs. I hope you have as much fun creating jewelry as I have!

tools & supplies

There are some fundamental tools and supplies you'll need to make the projects in this book. Having the right tools for any job, including scrapbooking and jewelry design, is essential. Most of the tools listed below are available through your local craft stores.

Basic tools

Many of these tools will be used often as you work on the projects in this book. I suggest you gather these tools before you begin crafting. Keep the tools in a safe place so you can find them quickly when you're ready to begin crafting.

[awl]

The sharp point of an awl creates a hole through many types of items without destroying the area around the hole. Use the awl over a self-healing mat to protect your work surface.

[eyelet setter]

A wonderful scrapbook tool used to secure eyelets to holes in paper and ribbon. Use the eyelet setter over a self-healing mat to protect your work surface.

[hammer]

Used with an awl to create small holes in scrapbook elements, and with an eyelet setter to set eyelets.

[hole punch]

This item creates holes in paper and laminated plastic for eyelets and other uses. Comes in a variety of sizes.

[long-nose pliers]

These pliers have a longer end that may be serrated. Serrated ends grip better but may mar the surface of the object they hold. They are great for opening and closing jump rings or wire loops and straightening wire as well.

[round-nose pliers]

These pliers have smooth, rounded and tapered ends that are ideal for making curves or loops in wire. Westrim Crafts makes an excellent set of long and round-nose pliers.

[wire cutters]

Used to cut wire and snip off bits of metal. These are safer and easier to use than scissors for cutting wire. I used a pair of Westrim Crafts wire cutters for this book.

[craft knife]

The sharp razor blade point is useful for cutting paper and cardstock, and in a variety of other crafting techniques.

[scissors]

It's helpful to keep a sharp pair of all-purpose scissors and a small pair of manicure scissors on hand for these projects.

[jeweler's file]

A small, fine file that can be used for smoothing the edges of metal.

[paintbrush]

Very useful for applying primer, paint, pigment powder or varnish.

[sanding sponge]

A soft sanding pad used for preparing surfaces for primer.

[heat embossing tool]

A portable heat gun for crafting. Used to cure the liquid goop in the image transfer technique (see page 13).

If you have questions about the use of any product, try calling the product's customer service line. It allows you to get the most from your tools. Turn to page 78 for contact information.

tip

Adhesives

The right adhesives are essential to every project. Some adhesives work better on certain surfaces than others, so choosing a glue can be tricky when you want to glue two different types of surfaces together. The adhesive must work for both surfaces. It's important to read the directions or call the manufacturer if you have questions. I highly recommend the following adhesives.

[paper glue]

Aleene's 2 in 1 Glue is an effective adhesive for paper-to-paper surfaces. This glue should be familiar to scrapbookers.

[craft glue]

Aleene's Fast Grab Tacky Glue is a great glue for combining surfaces such as paper and metal or paper and wood together.

[embellishment glue]

Aleene's Platinum Bond Glass & Bead Slick Surfaces is excellent for bead work, but it works on other surfaces as well. Glass, Metal & More Permanent Glue is another good glue for slick surfaces such as metals, glass and jewelry. Beacon's Quick Grip All-Purpose Permanent Adhesive is a great, multipurpose glue that sets up quickly and firmly.

[double-sided craft tape]

Another useful product for adhering paper elements together. Make sure to use only double-sided craft tape, and not regular double-sided tape.

Primers & sealers

Primers and sealers are another key element to a successful scrapbook jewelry project. Without the proper primer and sealer, your project can end up chipping or bubbling and the end result can be unpredictable.

[metal primer]

Metal surfaces to be painted should be lightly sanded, wiped off and primed with a metal primer such as Delta's Ceramcoat Metal Primer. This will help the metal surface accept the paint or pigment powders.

[varnish]

Newly painted surfaces need a topcoat or two of varnish to protect the surface from light scratches and dirt. It's always worth the time to protect your work with a good varnish such as the Delta Ceramcoat Gloss Exterior/Interior Varnish.

[dimensional glaze]

Topcoats for paper can be a little tricky. You want a transparent effect and you don't want to ruin the paper. Aleene's Paper Glaze is a familiar product in the scrapbooking world and a good sealer for paper products.

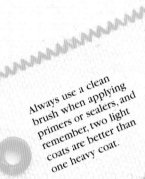

Always use a clean brush when applying primers or sealers, and remember, two light coats are better than one heavy coat.

tip

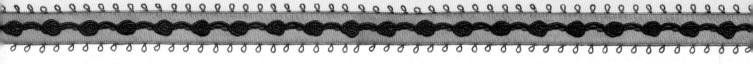

materials

I've used a number of jewelry and scrapbook materials to create the projects in this book. Understanding how these products work will help you in your own designs.

Scrapbook materials

Many scrapbook materials can be used to make jewelry. Listed below are just a few of the most common ones we will be using, though a browse through the scrapbooking section in any store will reveal a wealth of other exciting products. You can find scrapbook materials in scrapbook stores as well as most craft stores.

[paper]
Scrapbook paper comes in a variety of colors and styles. You can even find papers with textures, such as suede and ribbing.

[eyelet]
Eyelets are used in jewelry projects to secure holes in ribbon and keep them from fraying, to secure paper, to keep laminate from tearing and to create a finished look for a hole in metal.

[brad]
Brads are used to anchor washers and embellishments to larger scrapbook jewelry pieces, and to anchor spacer beads for a decorative touch to a jewelry design.

[photo anchor]
Normally used to secure photographs on scrapbook pages, they can also be used to add glimmer and dangle to a jewelry piece.

[slide]
A tiny buckle used to decorate scrapbook pages, a slide is used in the design of layered scrapbook elements, but it makes an excellent decorative accent as well.

[concho]
An embellishment with prongs underneath to help attach it to a surface.

[washer]
A decorative round metal element with a large hole in the center.

[hang tag]
A metal frame with a loop at the top. They make an excellent base for many jewelry projects.

[decorative link]
A metal frame with a loop on each end. This is another product that makes an excellent base for jewelry projects such as bracelets.

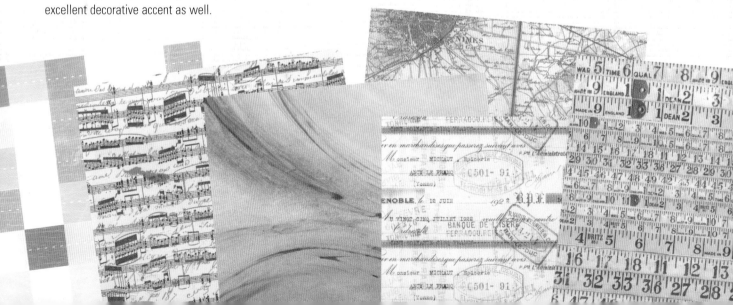

Jewelry materials

Jewelry findings are the materials that help finish a jewelry piece. Without the right clasp or finding, you risk a project failing. Jewelry findings can be found at craft stores everywhere.

[jump ring]
Small ring of wire with a seam you can open and close with pliers. They are used to hook and secure jewelry findings together.

[spring ring]
Clasp end for a necklace or bracelet that can be opened or closed with a sliding spring lever.

[toggle clasp]
Clasp set in which one end of the clasp (t-shaped) fits through the other end (circular-shaped).

[ear wire]
Refers to a kidney-shaped finding that passes through the ear to make earrings.

[head pin]
A stiff, straight wire with a flat head at one end, used for threading beads.

[eye pin]
A stiff, straight wire with a small loop at one end, used for threading beads.

[pin back]
Metal hardware used to attach a pin to your clothing.

[wire]
The projects in this book call for 20-gauge and 24-gauge craft wire. The higher the gauge, the thinner the wire and the more pliable it is. Both of these are easy to work with and are available at craft stores.

Beads

There are many types of beads, and those beads go by many names in the jewelry industry. If you can't find a particular bead listed in a project's material list, look for something similar. Here are a few bead descriptions. Please note these describe bead shapes, not the material. Beads can be made of materials such as glass, metal, acrylic, clay and more.

[rondelle beads]
Rondelle beads are often called spacer beads and are flatter than other beads. These beads have larger holes than usual.

[tube beads]
These beads are tube shaped. Otherwise, they can be of any color or design.

[seed beads]
Very small round beads. They are inexpensive and come in a variety of colors and a range of opening sizes.

[bugle beads]
Very small tubular shape beads that come in a variety of lengths and colors.

[crimp beads]
Small metal beads that are threaded onto jewelry wire and crushed in place with pliers to secure pieces on the wire.

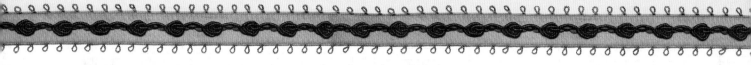

techniques

Learning the following basic techniques will make it possible to create the projects in this book. Don't be afraid to experiment and create new techniques of your own.

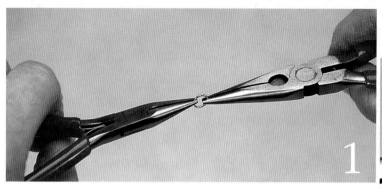

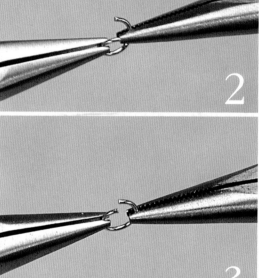

Opening & closing jump rings

There actually is a right way and a wrong way to open and close jump rings. The right way will give you a closer fit and not damage the jump ring.

[one] To open a jump ring, grip each side of the jump ring opening with a pair of long-nose pliers.

[two] Twist the ring, rolling one wrist forward and the other wrist backward.

[three] To close the jump ring, hold each side of the ring with long-nose pliers and roll your wrists back until the wires of the jump ring touch.

Coiling wire

Coiling wire is a simple process and creates a wonderful accent for your jewelry designs. Coiled spirals can be tight with the wire close together, or loose with space between the wire. Sometimes you can loosen a coil with your fingers and adjust the space without using pliers.

[one] Use round-nose pliers to begin the coil. Start at one end of the wire. Hold the wire in the pliers and rotate your wrist clockwise.

[two] Use long-nose pliers to finish the coil. Continue rotating your wrist clockwise until you are satisfied with the size of the coil.

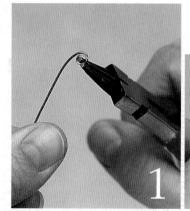

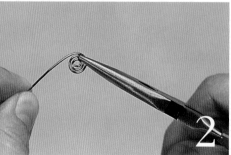

Using an awl & hammer

My favorite secret weapons in jewelry making, especially scrapbook jewelry making, are an awl and hammer. The sharp point of an awl helps to gently create a hole without damaging the project. I start with gentle taps to test how the material is responding before I use solid taps of the hammer.

[**one**] Mark the place on the scrapbook element where you want to make a hole. Mark the hole in the front of the scrapbook element so the rough edges will be in the back when you make the hole.

[**two**] Place the awl on the mark and begin to hammer the top of the awl.

[**three**] Widen the hole by hammering from the back. Repeat, going from front to back and hammering carefully, until the hole is large enough. You can also widen the hole by twisting the element back and forth down the shaft of the awl.

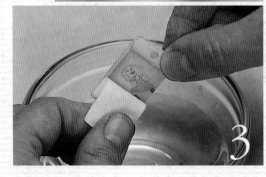

Transferring images

There are many image transfer techniques, but this is my favorite because the medium used dries to a rubber-like substance that's scratch- and UV ray-resistant. Before using this product from Transfers Unlimited by Artisan's Choice (or any product for the first time), review the package instructions.

[**one**] Copy the image using an ink-jet printer. Heat the paper in a toaster oven for two minutes to remove all moisture, then let it cool for a minute. Brush a thick layer of transfer medium over the image and the surrounding embellishment.

[**two**] Place the image back in the oven and bake for an additional three minutes. Remove, then heat the image with an embossing tool until the surface is glossy. When it's cool, trim the excess paper and soak it in water for 20 minutes.

[**three**] Peel the paper backing from the transferred image.

1

embellishments everywhere!

There is an unlimited array of scrapbook embellishments waiting to be used in your jewelry projects. Decorative metal paper clips become the base for a gorgeous lapel pin that shows a sense of smart style. Letter brads give an elegant ribbon bracelet a whole new meaning, while hang tags and decorative washers add class to a pair of earrings.

Easy-to-follow steps will allow you to replicate the designs and create fabulous jewelry. Experiment with your own creative touches and be inspired by the ideas in every project. Enjoy the many opportunities these creative embellishments give the clever crafter!

beaded frame **necklace**

Think outside the box! Convert a bracelet frame into a necklace. Rather than fill the frame with stickers, use tiny marbles and gorgeous beads for a textured look. Scrapbook photo anchors and brads add finishing touches to the design. This bracelet is a pleasure to make and undeniably beautiful.

what you need

Silver round frame bracelet
ARTchix Studio

Tiny red marbles mix

Gold photo anchors

Small gold brads

18" (46cm) silver chain necklace

Silver and gold jump rings

Embellishment glue

Long-nose pliers

Wire cutters

Small container, such as a cup

Toothpick

inspiring **ideas**

Don't be afraid to experiment with tiny marble combinations. Why not add some seed beads and bugle beads? Mix a few of your left-over beads and see what you can create.

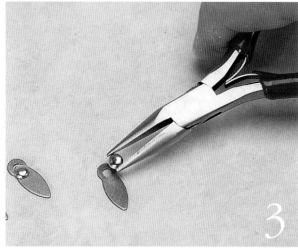

[one] Remove the clasp ends from the frame bracelet. Snip the necklace chain into two equal pieces using wire cutters. Adjust the chain to the desired length, keeping it longer if you want a longer frame necklace and shorter for a choker. Attach the chains to either end of the frame bracelet using jump rings. The clasp ends for the necklace should be at either end of the chains.

[two] Spread a thick coat of adhesive into one frame. Use a toothpick to make sure the adhesive reaches the edges of the frame. Hold the frame over a container and gently pour the tiny marbles mix into the frame until the frame is filled. Pour the excess tiny marbles back into a cup, then repeat this procedure with each additional frame. Let the frames dry overnight.

[three] Cut the ends off a gold brad using wire cutters. Glue the brad head to a gold photo anchor, slightly overlapping the hole in the anchor with the brad head. Repeat for each gold photo anchor. Let these dry overnight.

[four] Attach silver jump rings between each beaded frame. Attach a second silver jump ring to the first. Attach the gold photo anchors to the second silver jump rings using gold jump rings.

charm slide **earrings**

Hang tags are the perfect base to show off the stunning metal embellishments you can find in the scrapbook market. Layer the embellishments for a look that has depth and interest. If you can't find these same embellishments in your local store, experiment with other combinations to find a design that suits your style.

what you need

Silver mini hang tags
Nunn Design

Copper Ribbon Details
Traditional slides
Nunn Design

Gold decorative washers
Jest Charming Embellishments

Silver mini brads

Gold ear wires

Long-nose pliers

Round-nose pliers

Awl

Hammer

Pencil

Ruler

inspiring **ideas**

Look for hang tags in different shapes such as circles and rectangles. Then try embellishing them with painted scrapbook washers, decorative brads, or scrapbook charms for other unique earring designs.

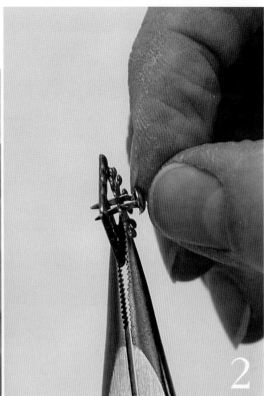

[**one**] Find the center of a square mini hang tag by drawing diagonal lines from opposite corners of the square. Where the lines meet will be the center of the tag. On a protected surface, punch a hole in the center of the mini hang tag using a hammer and awl.

[**two**] Assemble the center of the earring. Thread a washer onto a brad, and then thread the center bar of a copper slide on the brad. Use long-nose pliers to help assemble the earring.

[**three**] Thread the brad ends through the center hole in the tag. Coil each brad end under itself using round-nose pliers.

[**four**] Open the loop at the bottom of the ear wire with long-nose pliers. Thread the hang tag onto the loop, then close the loop. Repeat this entire process for the second earring.

wire and bead **stickpin**

The nostalgic T-pin embellishments you can find in stores are a reminder of the stickpins our grand-mothers wore many years ago, but with a modern twist. Add all kinds of things such as glass beads, buttons, wire and charms to personalize and make the pin uniquely your own. Wear it on your favorite scarf, blazer, coat or beret.

what you need

Nostalgiques T-Pin
EK Success #RSNA009

Glass goldstone beads mix

Gold metal bead tube

Gold metal rondelle bead

Gold love charms
Blue Moon Beads

Silver-lined red rochaille beads

Gold head pins

20-gauge gold wire

Embellishment glue

Long-nose pliers

Round-nose pliers

Wire cutters

Ruler

Toothpick

inspiring **ideas**

Design your T-pin stickpin to be worn horizontally if you like. Or mount a pin on the front of a card for a quick gift.

20

[one] Wrap the center of a 5"
(13cm) long gold wire a few times
around the top of the T-pin. Coil the
wire ends using round-nose pliers.
Thread a gold bead tube on the T-pin.

[two] Thread a gold rondelle bead
on the T-pin. Cut and thread a 5" (13cm)
wire halfway through the gold rondelle
bead. Coil each end of the wire using
round-nose pliers.

[three] Thread a square
red goldstone bead and rondelle
bead on the T-pin. Cut and
thread a 3" (8cm) gold wire
halfway through the gold
rondelle bead. Wrap the lower
half of the wire around the
T-pin below the rondelle bead.
Thread one red rochaille bead
on the upper half of the wire
and coil the wire end.

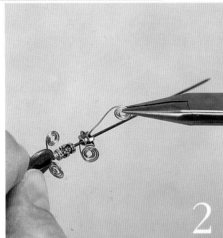

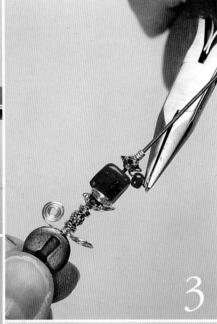

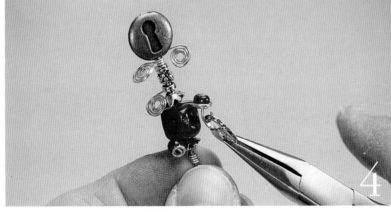

[four] Thread a red rochaille bead on a head pin. Cut off the excess wire,
leaving 1/8" (3mm) of wire on the end. Thread the beaded headpin through the
bottom coil on the right side, with the bead on top. Bend the wire below the coil
into a loop using round-nose pliers. Attach the gold lock charm to the loop, and
close the loop using long-nose pliers.

[five] Thread another red rochaille bead on a head pin. Cut off the excess
wire, leaving 1/8" (3mm) of wire on the end. Thread the head pin through the
top coil on the left side. Bend the wire end into a loop and attach the key charm,
using long-nose pliers; close the loop. Finish by adjusting the heights and posi-
tions of the coils with long-nose pliers as desired. To hold the elements in place,
apply a small amount of embellishment glue to the wrapped wires at the top
and bottom of the T-pin using a toothpick.

red hot flower **earrings**

This earring project uses beads in a traditional way (threaded on wires) and acrylic scrapbook flowers in a nontraditional way (in jewelry instead of on paper). The acrylic flowers sparkle next to the gold and red beads stacked high on the head pins. It makes a bold statement, but it is simple to construct.

what you need

Icicles Red Hot Flowers
KI Memories #842

Gold corrugated ring spacers

6mm dark red confetti beads

Dark red oval confetti beads

Gold metal rondelle beads

3mm gold-plated beads

Gold spacers

Gold head pins

Gold post with ball and drop earring findings

Gold jump rings

Long-nose pliers

Round-nose pliers

Wire cutters

inspiring ideas

If you'd rather see the front of your scrapbook embellishment (instead of the edge, as shown here), get some inspiration from the projects on pages 26 and 48.

22

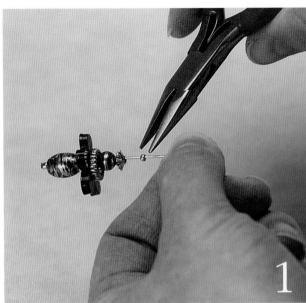

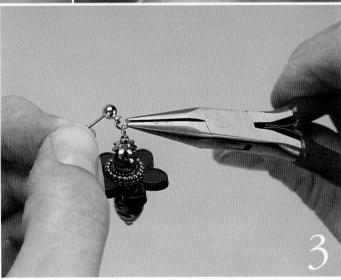

[one] Thread the following items on a head pin: 3mm gold bead, oval confetti bead, gold spacer, red hot flower, 3mm gold bead, gold corrugated ring spacer, 6mm confetti bead, gold rondelle and 3mm gold bead.

[two] Push the decorative items toward the end of the head pin. Snip off excess wire using wire cutters, leaving 1/4" (6mm) at the end. Coil a loop at the end of the wire using round-nose pliers.

[three] With a jump ring, attach a gold post with a ball drop to the earring, using long-nose pliers. Repeat these steps to make the second red flower earring.

letter brad **ribbon bracelet**

Mixing decorative brads with fabric—ribbon, in this case—is one new way to use this exciting embellishment. Using letter brads allows you to add your own message. With this project, you'll be making a statement in no time!

what you need

My Type concho brad alphabet pieces
Colorbök

2' (61cm) red grosgrain ribbon, ³/₄" (19mm) wide

Black embroidery thread

Small silver brads

Silver eyelets

Silver toggle clasp

6mm silver jump rings

Eyelet setter

Hammer

Long-nose pliers

Round-nose pliers

Sewing needle

Straight pins

Small craft scissors

Ruler

inspiring **ideas**

Check out the numerous brad styles available, such as those with pictures or designs. Then use different colors of ribbon to create unique gifts for friends and family.

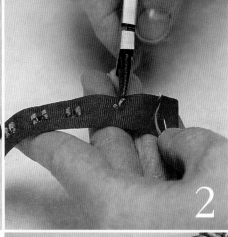

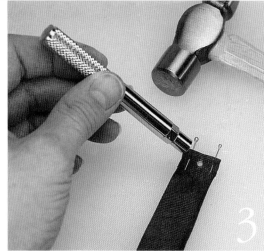

[one] Cut the ribbon into two pieces, each 7¹/₂" (19cm) long, and set one aside. Fold the ribbon end under ¹/₂" (13mm) on either end. Pin the ends in place. Find the center of the ribbon and space out the letter brads, leaving ¹/₁₆" (2mm) space between each brad.

[two] Attach one brad at a time by snipping a small slit in the ribbon where brad ends will pass through. Insert the brad, and coil each brad end with round-nose pliers. Attach each letter brad this way. Place a mark for one small silver brad on either end of the letter brads, approximately ³/₈" (9mm) away from the lettering. Snip a small slit at each mark for the silver brad ends to pass through and coil each brad end with round-nose pliers.

[three] Set the first ribbon on top of the second. Line up and pin one end of ribbon front and back together, with brads on the outside and the brad ends contained between the ribbons. At the pinned end, use small craft scissors to make a small slit through the layers of ribbon for an eyelet. Attach the eyelet using an eyelet setter and hammer on a protected surface.

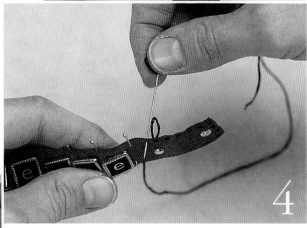

[four] Pin and stitch the front and back ribbons together with two strands of embroidery thread, starting around the attached eyelet and working toward the open end. When you're finished, attach the second eyelet to the other ribbon bracelet end.

[five] Attach a toggle clasp set to the eyelets with jump rings and long-nose pliers.

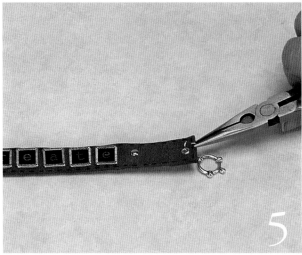

spiral bead **earrings**

Layering a variety of elements, such as decorative washers, paper clips, scrapbook spirals and glass beads, is the key to this design. Powdered pigment adds a splash of color to these gorgeous earrings that showcase the possibilities of scrapbook jewelry.

what you need

Green Czech glass teardrop beads

Gold clamshell earring finding

4mm gold jump rings

7mm gold jump rings

24-gauge gold wire

Jacquard Pearl Ex Duo Blue-Green Powdered Pigment
Rupert, Gibbon& Spider #681

Metal primer

In/Out Spirales
7gypsies

Gold decorative washers
Jest Charming Embellishments

Small drop pendants
ARTchix Studio

Triangle paper clips
Making Memories

Varnish

Embellishment glue

Small brush

Long-nose pliers

Wire cutters

Sanding sponge

Ruler

Toothpick

inspiring **ideas**

Try layering photo anchors or other decorative charms or jewelry findings to these scrapbook spirals. Or add some colorful beads to brighten the earrings even more.

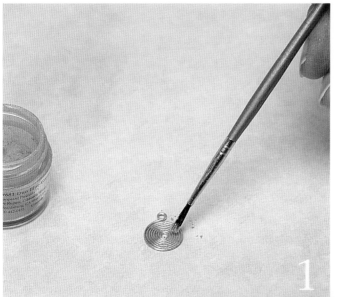

[one] Lightly sand and wipe off the surface of each spirale. Apply one coat of metal primer to each spirale. Let it dry. Apply one coat of varnish, then immediately brush the blue-green pigment powder on the spirale surface. Let it dry. Seal the surface with one or two coats of varnish.

[two] Attach a 4mm jump ring to the small drop pendant. Thread a 4" (10cm) gold wire through the center of the spirale. Bend and loop the wire downward, threading the jump ring onto the loop. Thread the wire through the spirale one additional time, trimming the excess wire from the backside of the spirale. Carefully press the wire flat using long-nose pliers.

[three] Spread a triangle paper clip open using long-nose pliers. Gently insert and press the ends into the green glass teardrop bead. Apply a small amount of adhesive to the bead openings using a toothpick.

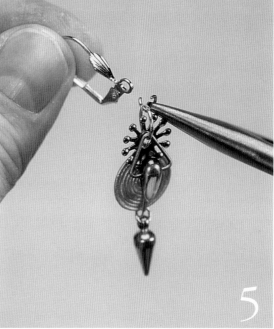

[four] Open a 7mm jump ring using long-nose pliers. Thread the top loop of the spirale, a decorative washer and the paper clip from step three onto the jump ring. Close the jump ring with long-nose pliers.

[five] Attach the 7mm jump ring to a clamshell earring finding using a 4mm jump ring and long-nose pliers. Repeat these procedures for the second earring.

star **pin**

A decorative metal paper clip becomes a sparkling three-dimensional lapel pin in this project. Metallic and glass beads add color, while metal coils add texture. It's the perfect complement to an outfit that needs a bit of sparkle.

what you need

Lil' Clips silver star clip
American Traditional Designs #LC-0016

Details gold star and mini gold star embellishments
Nunn Design #ddst

Silver metal large star beads

Gold Japanese glass square beads

4mm gold beads

3mm gold beads

Gold head pins

Silver eye pins

6mm silver jump rings

Gold pin back

Embellishment glue

Awl

Hammer

Round-nose pliers

Long-nose pliers

Wire cutters

inspiring ideas

Flat metal paper clips come in all different shapes and sizes. Check your local scrapbook store for unique and beautiful embellishments and beads for this project.

[one] Use an awl and hammer on a protected surface to punch a hole in the center of the gold star embellishment. Punch a hole near one point of the gold mini star embellishment, then punch a hole in the top center of a paper clip star and a hole in the top of the center strip of the clip.

[two] Thread a 4mm gold bead, a silver star bead and the gold star embellishment on a gold head pin. Insert the head pin through the hole in the paper clip star. Cut the excess wire, leaving a 1/8" (3mm) end. Bend the remaining wire end into a tight coil on the back of the pin, using round-nose pliers.

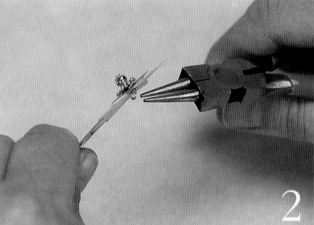

[three] Begin coiling the bottom of the center strip of the paper clip. Insert a head pin through the punched hole in the center strip. Thread the following beads onto the head pin: a 3mm gold bead, a silver star bead, gold square bead, a silver star bead and a 3mm gold bead. Cut the excess wire, leaving a 1/8" (3mm) end. Bend the wire end into a small loop, using round-nose pliers.

[four] Use long-nose pliers to attach a jump ring to the hole in the mini star embellishment and another jump ring to the loop on the head pin. Join the two jump rings to attach the star to the clip.

[five] Continue coiling the center strip until the beaded head pin dangles vertically against the front of the paper clip. Apply embellishment glue to the pin back and attach it vertically to the backside of the paper clip pin. Fit the tight coil from step two through the hole in the pin back to keep all the pieces secure.

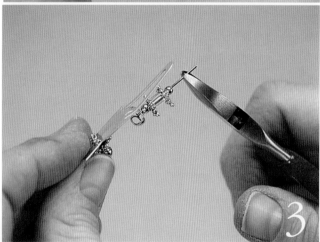

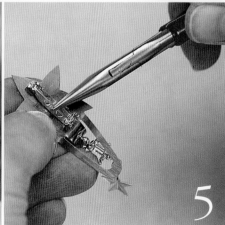

stars and slides **watchband**

Turn a plain watch into a gorgeous piece of jewelry with beautiful silver accents from the scrapbooking world. This project allows you to quickly create a functional and fabulous piece that it looks like it cost a fortune, but it didn't.

what you need

Watch with black leather straps and silver face

Silver Ribbon Details traditional slides
Nunn Design

Silver metal large star beads
Blue Moon Beads #52885

Nickel square conchos
Magic Scraps #466-NH

Silver mini brads

Craft knife

Long-nose pliers

Round-nose pliers

Wire cutters

inspiring ideas

Consider purchasing additional leather bands to decorate with scrapbook elements in other colors and shapes. Add accents of paint to the metal embellishments for a totally different look.

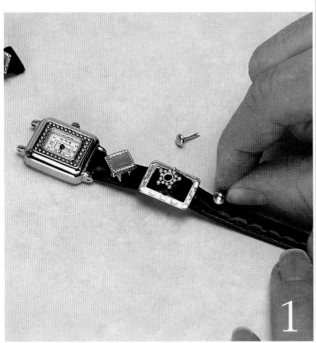

[one] Plan the placement of slides, beads, square conchos and brads on the straps of the watch. Remove the leather straps from the watch itself. Using wire cutters, trim the excess prongs that interfere with placement from the embellishments before you attach them to the leather straps.

[two] Place a concho on the watchband and begin pressing down the metal points of the concho's underside into the leather strap. Continue pressing until the points puncture the underside of the strap. Use the point of a craft knife to complete the puncture hole if necessary. Bend the points on the underside of the strap using long-nose pliers to secure the concho in place.

[three] Line up the slide on the watchband and make two tiny slits in the band on either side of the center bar of the slide. Thread a star bead on the brad and insert the brad ends into the tiny slits and through the leather band. Coil the brad ends using round-nose pliers. Insert a single brad into the watchband below the slide using a prepunched watchband hole or create a hole using a craft knife. Coil the brad ends under separately, using round-nose pliers.

[four] Once all the embellishments are secure, reattach the finished band to the watch.

nostalgic **clip pin**

Scrapbook decorative paper clips have wires that can be bent and manipulated into a variety of loops and designs, making them the perfect accompaniment to this design. Metal washers and a pin backing finish out a piece that is both artsy and stylish.

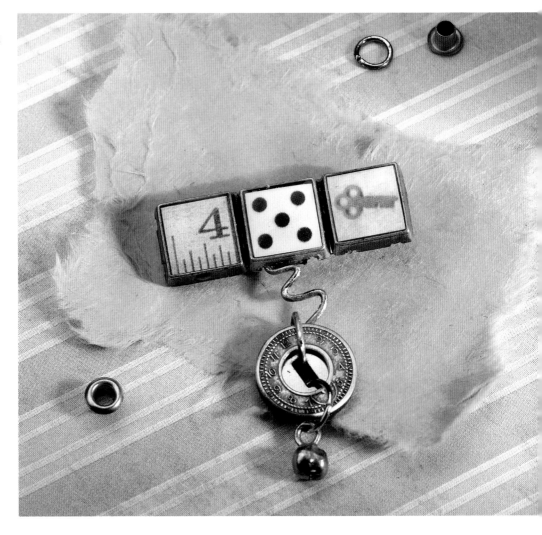

what you need

The Attic Collection paper clips by Nostalgiques
EK Success

The Attic Collection small self-adhesive washers by Nostalgiques
EK Success

Gold washers

5mm gold jewelry bell

7mm gold jump ring

1" (3cm) gold pin back

Piece of sturdy material for pin backing, such as thin cardboard or metal

Embellishment glue

Long-nose pliers

Round-nose pliers

Wire cutters

Jeweler's file

Scissors

Pencil

inspiring **ideas**

Try adding beads and other scrapbook elements to the new acrylic paper clips on the market. Practice bending regular paper clip wire into shapes first to get to know the feel (strength) of wire and how it can be manipulated.

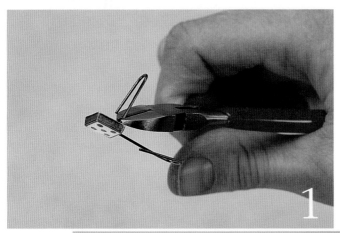

[one] Snip the paper clip wires off two of the paper clips. File rough edges with a jeweler's file. Snip the short paper clip wire off a third paper clip.

[two] Bend the long paper clip wire into a zigzag shape with long-nose pliers. Bend a large loop in the wire end using round-nose pliers.

[three] Sandwich one plain gold washer between two self-adhesive washers.

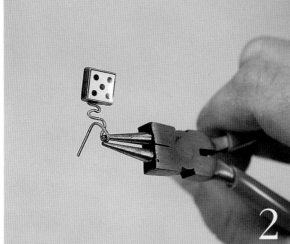

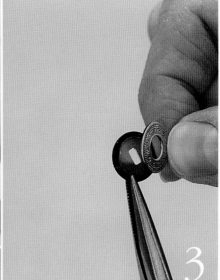

[four] Attach a jewelry bell to the washers with a jump ring, using long-nose pliers. Connect the washers to the paper clip wire loop.

[five] Lay the paper clips side by side on a sturdy backing. Trace their rectangular shape onto the backing, then cut out the shape. Glue the paper clips to the backing. Let the glue dry before you continue. When dry, glue the pin back to the back of the paper clip pin. Let it dry.

painted **key chain**

Sometimes the simplest enhancements are the prettiest. This stamped metal paper clip is enhanced by applying pigments over acrylic paint to create a shimmering, dimensional look that contrasts nicely against the shiny and brushed metals of the clip.

inspiring ideas

Try this technique on any imprinted metal scrapbook embellishments such as charms and tags.

[**one**] Punch a hole in the bottom of the paper clip using an awl and hammer on a protected surface. Enlarge the hole further by twisting the awl in the hole. Add a scrapbook eyelet to the hole using an eyelet setter and hammer on a protected surface.

[**two**] Attach a key chain split ring to a lanyard hook. Attach the lanyard hook to the hole in the paper clip.

[**three**] Lightly sand the raised metal areas of the paper clip where you will be painting. Brush away the dust before continuing.

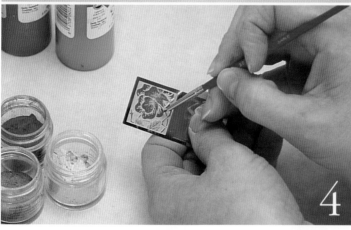

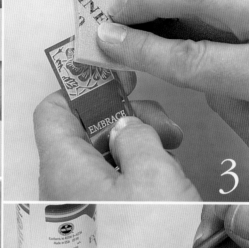

[**four**] Apply one coat of metal primer to the areas that are going to be painted. Let it dry. Apply one color of acrylic paint to the paper clip at a time. Immediately apply pigment powder with a dry brush over the wet paint for a unique, dimensional look. I used the following paint and pigment combinations:

- Flower petals: *Royal Fuchsia paint with Misty Lavender and Brilliant Gold pigment*
- Flower center: *Royal Fuchsia paint with True Blue pigment*
- Leaves: *Jubilee Green and Lime Green paint with Spring Green pigment*
- Stems: *Jubilee Green paint and Spring Green pigment*
- Lettering: *Royal Fuchsia paint*

[**five**] After the paint dries, apply two to three coats of gloss varnish over the painted areas of the paper clip, allowing drying time between coats.

putting your paper to use

How many times have you come across a simply stunning piece of paper and wished for the perfect project to showcase the find? Look no further, for you'll find projects like that in this section! Scrapbooking offers us a wealth of papers with a variety of textures, colors and designs. With the papers you love, you'll create everything from earrings, tie tacks, memento necklaces and more. New paper designs become available almost every day, so you'll never lack for inspiration to create new projects.

Thumb through the pages of fabulous papers you've collected as you browse through this collection of gorgeous projects.

laser-cut **earrings**

Combining layers of laser-cut tags with a favorite scrapbook collage paper gives this project an appealing and unique dimensional look, as if you're peering through a window at the artwork below. A gold bead adds a focal point and flair to this gorgeous project.

what you need

Laser-cut tag embellishments
Deluxe Designs #32-009

Seaside collage paper
NRN Designs #B12281

Glass foil beads mix

Silver-lined gold
rochaille beads

Gold head pins

6mm gold jump rings

Gold post with ball and drop earrings

Gold eyelets

Paper glue

Dimensional glaze

Eyelet setter

Hammer

1/8" (3mm) hole punch

Long-nose pliers

Round-nose pliers

Wire cutters

Scissors

Small brush

inspiring **ideas**

This is a fun way to utilize extra tag embellishments and left-over scrapbook paper. Use your imagination and try making jewelry from the paper scraps you have at home.

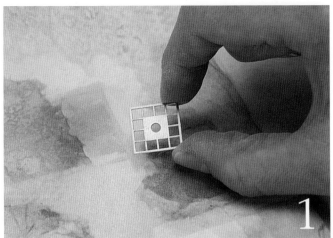

[one] Select four laser-cut tags of the same size. Choose an area of the scrapbook paper to highlight in your earrings. Adhere each tag to the front of the scrapbook paper using glue. Let dry. Apply dimensional glaze to the tags and scrapbook paper. Let dry.

[two] Cut each tag out of the paper. Glue two tags together, making sure the tags face out. Repeat for the second earring. Let dry.

[three] Punch a hole through one corner of each tag, then through the opposite corner. Apply an eyelet to each hole and set it using an eyelet setter and hammer on a protected surface.

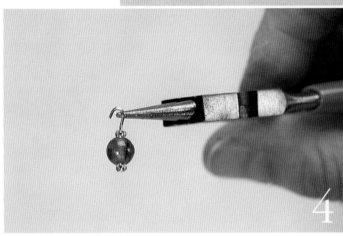

[four] Thread one gold rochaille bead, one mauve glass foil bead and one more gold rochaille bead on two separate head pins. Snip off excess head pin wire using wire cutters, leaving a 1/4" (6mm) wire end. Coil a loop on the end of each head pin using round-nose pliers.

[five] Attach the beaded head pins to the eyelets at the bottom of the squares using jump rings and long-nose pliers. Attach a gold post with a ball drop to each top eyelet using a jump ring and long-nose pliers.

charm **bracelet**

Create lovely charms using scrapbook paper, lamination and a gold leafing pen. Add them to a bracelet embellished with beads and you have a fabulous project that you finished in no time at all. Simple, but the results are stunning!

what you need

7" (18cm) gold charm bracelet

Green Japanese glass square beads

Gold metal beads

Gold head pins

6mm gold jump rings

Gold eyelets

18kt Gold leafing pen
Krylon

Eyelet setter

Real Life Paper Charms nature cardstock stickers
Pebbles, Inc. #36201

Meadow Green scrapbook paper
EK Success Ltd. #EKBPC106

Laminating kit (or use a commercial laminating service)

Hammer

1/8" (3mm) hole punch

Long-nose pliers

Round-nose pliers

Scissors

Wire cutters

inspiring **ideas**

Any paper can be laminated, so check your stash of scrap paper and find two or three papers to make your own charms. Try punching the paper in different shapes to make each unique.

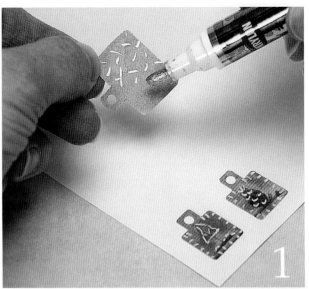

[**one**] Apply stickers to the back of the scrapbook paper. Highlight the stickers with the gold leafing pen. Cut out the stickers and highlight the scrapbook paper on the back of the charms with the gold leafing pen.

[**two**] Laminate the charms with a home laminating kit or at your local office supply store. Before lamination, place the charms face down on the adhesive side of the laminating sheet and decorate around the charms with dots from the gold leafing pen. Let the paint dry for a few minutes before finishing the laminating process. Lay the second sheet of laminate on top and laminate. Note: Laminating machines at office supply stores work at a very high temperature and may produce better results than a home laminating kit.

[**three**] Cut the charm shapes from the laminate and punch holes in the top of each charm using a 1/8" (3mm) hole punch. Insert a gold eyelet into each hole and set using an eyelet setter and hammer on a protected surface.

[**four**] Thread one gold bead between two green glass square beads on six separate head pins. Snip off the excess head pin wire, leaving a 1/4" (6mm) wire end. Coil a loop on the end of each head pin, using round-nose pliers.

[**five**] Lay the bracelet on your work surface, planning the placement of the charms and beaded head pins. Attach the charms and head pins with jump rings, using long-nose pliers.

Cut pieces of the laminate sheet a bit larger than each charm before applying them to the paper. You'll get much better results that way.

tip

bottle cap **necklace**

Scrapbook bottle caps are the whimsical focal point of this fun project. Lettering on decorative paper is glued to each bottle cap in a step that is sure to give meaning. This is an excellent project to do with kids, and it looks great with denim.

what you need

Green, red and purple bottle caps
ARTchix Studio

Create charm
Blue Moon Beads

Metal type paper images
ARTchix Studio

6mm silver-plated beads

Silver washers

Mixed jump rings

Silver head pins

Ball and chain necklace

Black permanent ink marker

Craft glue

Dimensional glaze

Awl

Hammer

Long-nose pliers

Round-nose pliers

Wire cutters

Metal file

Small paintbrush

Scissors

inspiring **ideas**

Instead of this design, try stringing the bottle caps straight across the chain. Using different words or adding embellishments other than words will give this necklace a very different feel.

[one] Cut the head off a head pin using wire cutters. Loop one end of the head pin wire using round-nose pliers. Thread a silver bead on the wire. Cut off the excess wire below the bead, leaving a 1/4" (6mm) wire end. Bend the wire end into a loop using round-nose pliers. Repeat this procedure to make four additional beaded wires.

[two] Thread one silver washer and one silver bead on a head pin. Cut off the excess wire, leaving a 1/4" (6mm) end. Bend the wire end into a loop using round-nose pliers.

[three] Find the center of the ball and chain necklace. Attach the silver-beaded head pin with a jump ring using long-nose pliers.

[four] Lay the necklace out, planning the placement of the bottle caps with beaded wire between them. Mark the bottle caps with a permanent ink marker where holes need to be made to connect bottle caps and beads together.

If you have trouble keeping the beads in place when laying out the necklace, lay the necklace on a piece of fabric such as felt

tip

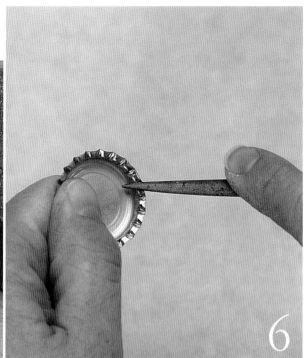

[**five**] Punch a small hole through each mark on the bottle caps using an awl and hammer on a protected surface.

[**six**] File the rough inside edges of the bottle cap with a metal file. Make sure there are no sharp edges that might touch the skin of the person wearing the necklace.

[**seven**] Use scissors to cut out the letters and glue them onto the bottle caps. Let dry. Paint two coats of dimensional glaze over each bottle cap's surface, allowing the caps to dry between coats.

Practice creating a hole on a spare bottle cap first. Tap the awl with the hammer very carefully. Place the bottle cap against a heavy object, such as a brick, to keep it from sliding across the work surface. **tip**

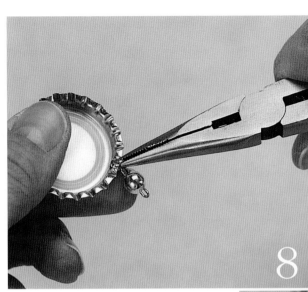

[**eight**] Connect the bottle caps to the beaded wires using jump rings and long-nose pliers.

[**nine**] Connect the bottle caps and beads to the ball and chain necklace using jump rings.

[**ten**] Connect the *Create* charm to the bottom beaded wire with a jump ring.

gentlemen's **tie tack**

Creating masculine jewelry can be a challenge, but it doesn't have to be. Rub-on transfers and metal scrapbook elements combine in this project for definite masculine appeal. This is an excellent gift for the men in your life.

what you need

Copper mini hang tag
Nunn Design

Butterfly clutch & tie tack set
Westrim Crafts

Fleur Decorative Details charm
Nunn Design

Bits of Time rub-on transfer
American Traditional Designs #RO-1022

White or ivory scrap cardstock

Craft glue

Embellishment glue

Dimensional glaze

Scissors

Wire cutters

Jeweler's file

Paintbrush

inspiring **ideas**

There are plenty of scrapbook accessories that have been designed with men in mind. Use them to create a tie tack like this one, cuff links or a key chain.

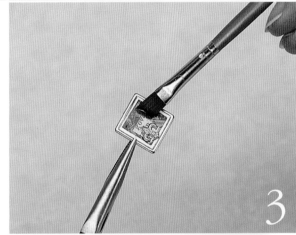

[one] Snip the loop off the hang tag. File the frame edge until smooth.

[two] Using the template that accompanied the hang tag, select and cut out a rub-on transfer. Apply the transfer to the cardstock, following the package directions. Cut out a smaller rub-on transfer and apply it to the lower-left corner of the transfer on cardstock.

[three] Cut out the cardstock transfer and glue it to the hang tag using embellishment glue. Attach the fleur charm to the hang tag using embellishment glue. Let it dry, then apply two coats of dimensional glaze to the transfer and charm, allowing drying time between coats.

[four] Apply the tie tack finding to the back of the charm using embellishment glue. Let it dry.

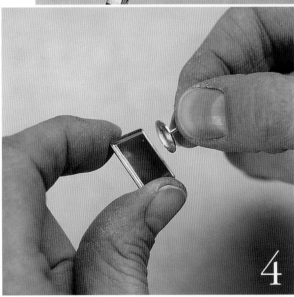

beads and wire **earrings**

Who would have thought combining epoxy donuts, scrapbook washers and wire would create such a unique look that's nostalgic, yet modern as well? Amber glass beads are a wonderful accent to the stickers. It's a simple project that appears to be anything but simple.

what you need

Long-nose pliers
Round-nose pliers
Wire-cutters
Ruler

Nostalgiques Botanical epoxy donuts
EK Success Ltd.

Gold washers

Amber-colored glass beads

20-gauge gold wire

Gold wire earring findings

inspiring ideas

Epoxy donut stickers come in a variety of colors, shapes and patterns. They are a great creative base for designing earrings, bracelets, pins or necklaces. Experiment with different papers, embellishments and surface treatments.

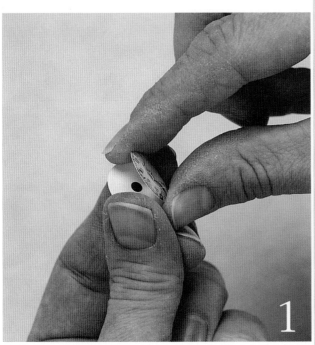

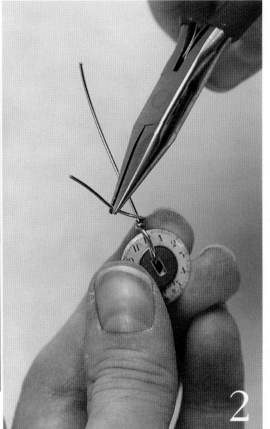

[one] Select two sets of epoxy donut stickers for the front and back of the earrings, four stickers total. Line up and press the donuts together.

[two] Cut two 4" (10cm) pieces of wire for each earring. Thread one wire through a donut, add washers on either side of the donut, and bend the wires upward. Wrap one end of the wire around the other at the top of the donut and trim only that end of the wire.

[three] Thread the second wire through the donut center and bend the wires over and downward. Wrap one end of the wire around the other, and trim that end of the wire only. Thread one amber bead on the other wire end. Cut off the excess wire, leaving a 1" (3cm) end. Coil the end using round-nose pliers.

[four] Cut the remaining wire at the top of each earring, leaving a 1/4" (6mm) end. Coil this end into a loop, and attach each earring to an ear wire using long-nose pliers.

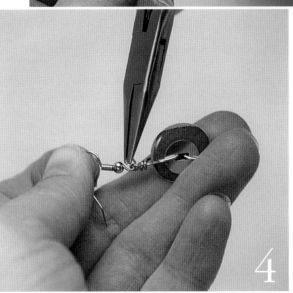

collage tag **bracelet**

This bracelet is a favorite project of mine. It combines beautiful colors and creativity for a stunning look. Decorative links are the base of this project, while collage tags add a splash of color and pattern. Mini brads are a stylish accent for the finished piece.

inspiring **ideas**

These decorative links are great for creating bracelets, earrings, necklaces and pins. Link them as shown here, use them singly with charms or beads attached to the loops or cut the loops off completely.

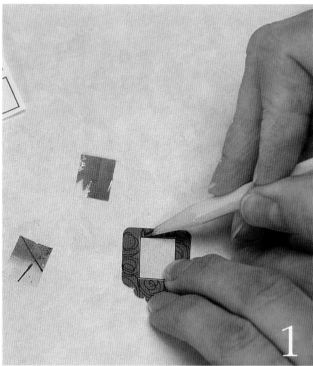

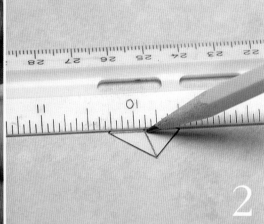

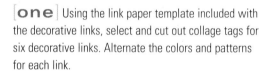

[one] Using the link paper template included with the decorative links, select and cut out collage tags for six decorative links. Alternate the colors and patterns for each link.

[two] Find the center of the paper link template by making a diagonal line from each corner to the opposite corner on the template using a ruler and pencil. Where the lines cross is the center.

[three] Lay the template on top of each link and punch a hole through the center of the link using an awl and hammer on a protected surface.

[four] Lay the collage tags on the links and punch a hole in each tag, using the hole you made in the previous step as a guide. Start the hole with a pencil in the back, and then finish the hole with a craft knife from the front.

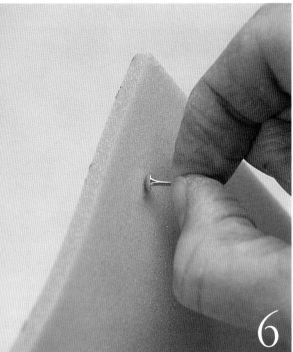

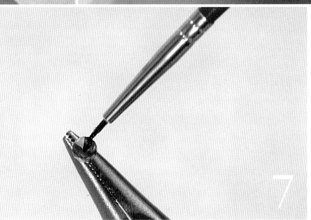

[five] Glue the collage tags to the surface of the link using craft glue. Let dry. Cover the tag surface with several coats of dimensional glaze, allowing drying time between coats.

[six] Lightly sand the heads of the brads with a sanding sponge.

[seven] Paint the brads with one coat of metal primer and let them dry, then paint the brads with multiple colors of acrylic paint. Follow with two coats of varnish, allowing drying time between coats.

When painting the brads, match the colors to those on the tags. Try using three different colors for each brad. And don't be afraid to paint abstract lines and swirls.

tip

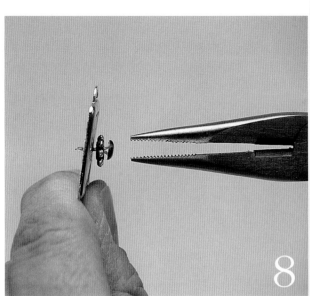

[eight] Insert the painted brads and gold and silver spacers in the center of each decorative link.

[nine] Coil each of the brad ends under the tags, using round-nose pliers.

[ten] Connect the the decorative links together using jump rings and long-nose pliers. Make sure all the pieces are face up.

[eleven] Use long-nose pliers and jump rings to attach a spring ring clasp set to either end of the bracelet.

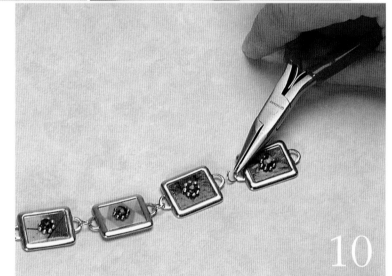

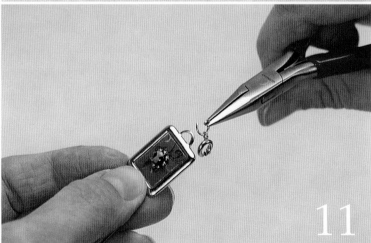

memento **necklace**

While hinge-top frames are commonly used for embellishing scrapbook pages, they can be cleverly used to make necklaces to honor a special occasion or event. This project converts one such frame into a holder for a collection of items representing a trip to France.

what you need

Brass hinge-top frame necklace kit
ARTchix Studio

Brass French Eiffel Tower charm
ARTchix Studio

Paris Librarie Layers transparencies
7gypsies

French coin

Gold spacer bead

Gold eyelet

8mm gold jump rings

Gold spring ring clasp set

24-gauge gold wire

Clear transparency film

White paper

3/16" (5mm) thick white foam board (stacked cardboard will also work)

Double-sided craft tape

Eyelet setter

Hammer

1/8" (3mm) hole punch

Long-nose pliers

Wire cutters

Scissors

Pencil

Ruler

inspiring **ideas**

The French coin used here is a personal memento from a trip to France. To make your necklace truly unique, use items such as pressed flowers, antique lace or coins from a special moment in your life.

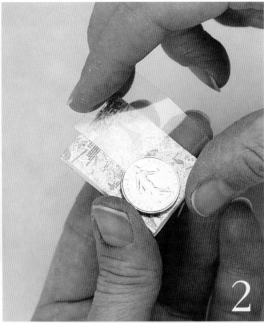

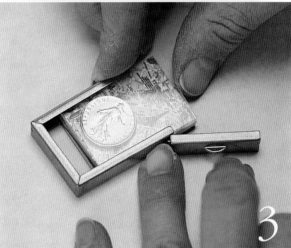

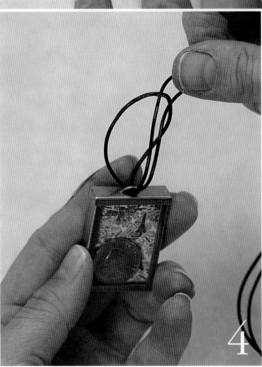

[one] Create a pattern for the necklace on a piece of white paper by tracing around the inside of the hinge-top frame. Cut outside the lines of the pattern. Use this pattern to cut a piece of foam-core board, then cut two pieces of clear transparency film and two pieces of the Paris street map transparency.

[two] To assemble the interior, lay the Paris street map transparencies on either side of the foam-core board. Lay the clear transparency on the back of the foam-core board, and the French coin on the front. Lay the other clear transparency over the coin.

[three] Slide the assembled pieces into the hinge-top frame and close the top.

[four] Bend the leather lace found in the necklace kit in half and thread the bend through the loop on the hinge box. Thread the two leather lace ends through the bend and pull tight.

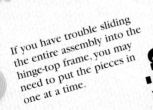

If you have trouble sliding the entire assembly into the hinge-top frame, you may need to put the pieces in one at a time. tip

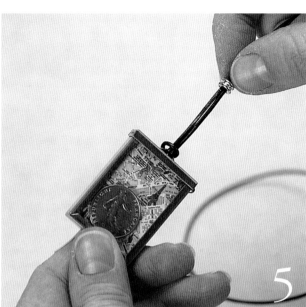

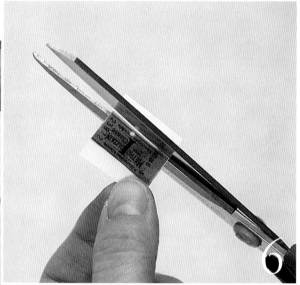

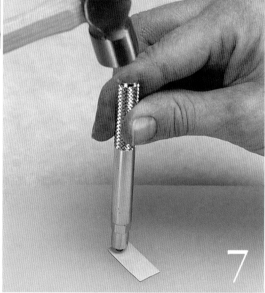

[**five**] Thread one gold spacer bead down both strands of the leather lace to the knot above the hinge-top frame.

[**six**] Cut out the Paris ticket transparency and adhere it to a white piece of paper using double-sided tape. Cut off the excess paper.

[**seven**] Punch a hole in the top of the ticket. Insert a gold eyelet into the hole and set using an eyelet setter and hammer on a protected surface.

[**eight**] Attach the Paris ticket and Eiffel Tower charm to the loop of leather lace using a large jump ring and long-nose pliers.

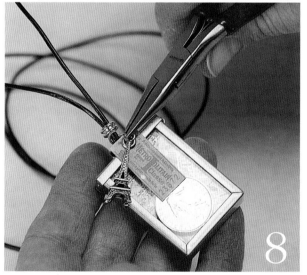

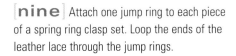

[nine] Attach one jump ring to each piece of a spring ring clasp set. Loop the ends of the leather lace through the jump rings.

[ten] Cut two pieces of wire 4" (10cm) long. Wrap the wire over the looped leather lace, starting beside the jump ring and going down the loop.

[eleven] Crush the end of the wrapped wire with the long-nose pliers to secure. Trim any excess leather lace and wire.

3

images, photos
pictures & more

New techniques and technology are being developed every year for our crafting use, and

I'm continually amazed by the products that are available to us. The wealth of

products for crafting with images and photos is

especially amazing! In this chapter, we'll be using some of those fantastic

products, such as transparencies, image transfer products, computers and color printers,

and more. Some of these new products can seem challenging, but they are simpler to

use than you might imagine, and the results are incredible. You'll

create bracelets that incorporate a child's cherished artwork, pendants with a favorite

photo, gorgeous frames for a wearable keepsake photo and a charm bracelet that is

uniquely yours. Enjoy letting your imagination run free as you

explore the projects in this section.

beaded photo **pin**

How better to honor photographs of the past than by putting them in a keepsake frame pin? This frame would normally be used on a scrapbook page, but it really comes to life as piece of wearable art. You can use this project to make wonderful Mother's Day gifts or pins for family reunions.

what you need

Antique photo

Rectangular frame charm
Daisy D's #7093 Elements

Gold glitter

Tiny gold marbles

Tiny gold metal tassel

6mm gold jump ring
Gold pin back

Clear transparency film

Thin piece of cardboard

Black permanent ink marker

Double-sided craft tape

Masking tape

Embellishment glue

Long-nose pliers

Scissors

Color copier

Pencil

Small container

inspiring
ideas

Consider using pressed flowers or postage stamps in the frame, or using a lace background instead of the beads.

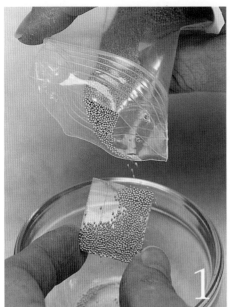

[one] Use the rectangular frame charm as a pattern to cut a piece of thin cardboard to slide into the frame. Using a permanent black marker, trace the pattern three times on a sheet of transparency film. Cut out these transparency pieces. Cover one of the transparencies with double-sided tape. Remove the tape backing, lay the transparency in a small container and sprinkle it with gold marbles and glitter.

[two] Make a color copy of your antique photo, reducing the image to approximately 1/8" (3mm) smaller than the frame size. Cut out the color photocopy, place tape on the back on the copy, and tape it to the center of one of the transparency pieces.

[three] Sandwich the transparency with the photocopy between the gold marbled transparency and the remaining clear transparency, with the photo and marbles facing forward. Lay this on the thin cardboard. Slide the stack into the frame charm.

[four] Crimp the tabs on the back and sides of the frame charm using long-nose pliers to secure the pieces inside the frame.

[five] Attach the gold metal tassel to the bottom loop of the frame charm with a jump ring and long-nose pliers. Glue the pin back to the cardboard on the back of frame charm using embellishment glue. Let the glue dry before using the pin.

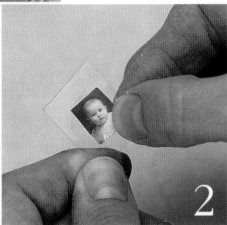

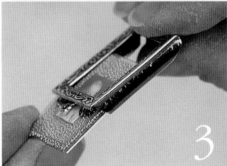

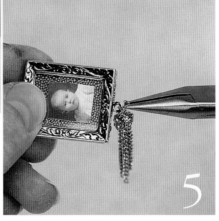

When crimping the frame edge, wrap masking tape around the tips of your long-nose pliers to prevent scratch marks on the frame.

tip

photo **pendant**

This project uses an image transfer technique to create a sharp, glossy reproduction of your favorite photograph. This unique process actually embeds the image into the scrapbook label holder frame, creating a "one of a kind" jewelry conversation piece.

what you need

Favorite photograph

Transfers Unlimited kit
Artisan's Choice

Aluminum oval label holder
Making Memories

Matte glass ocean beads mix

Silver decorative washer
Jest Charming Embellishments

Silver plain washers

Silver head pins

Silver jump rings

Barbell chain

Clear transparency film

Epson glossy photo paper

White Paint for Plastic
Plaid Enterprises, Inc.

Black permanent ink marker

Long-nose pliers

Round-nose pliers

Craft knife

Scissors

Wire cutters

Nail file

Heat embossing tool

Large paintbrush

Color copier or ink jet printer

Toaster oven or oven

Aluminum foil

Craft stick

Paper towels

Small pan to hold water

inspiring **ideas**

Try hanging the label holder horizontally with chains connected to both ends of the holder for a unique necklace or bracelet.

[one] Write your message on a transparency film using the black permanent ink marker and tape the transparency on the original photo, placing it where you would like the message on the pendant. To avoid damaging the photo, place the tape only on the outer edge of the photo.

[two] Using the copier, reduce or enlarge the photo to fit the label holder; make the copy onto Epson glossy ink-jet paper. I can't guarantee the project's success with any other brand of paper; I've tried others that didn't work. Cut out the image from the paper, leaving a 2" (5cm) margin around the image. Make sure the photo fits properly in the label holder when cropped (see Tip below).

[three] Read the instructions for the transfer medium, and consult the Transferring Images technique on page 13. Preheat your toaster oven to 325°F (163°C). Line the pan with aluminum foil. Heat the color copy for approximately two minutes to remove any moisture, then let it cool for one minute. Leave the photo on the toaster oven pan. Stir the transfer medium thoroughly with a craft stick and brush a thick layer of medium over the image and the surrounding area.

[four] Immediately lay the label holder over the image and into the medium. Brush additional medium over the image, label holder and surrounding area until all is fully engulfed by the medium.

Before starting, make sure the shape of your original photograph is compatible with the shape of the label holder. The size of the original can be reduced or enlarged on the copier.

tip

[five] Place the pendant back in the oven to bake for an additional three minutes. Remove from the oven and place it in a well-ventilated and heat-resistant area such as the stove top. Heat the image, label holder and surrounding area with a heat embossing tool. Watch for the medium surface to become glossy (a sign that the medium has cured). A nontoxic white smoke will be emitted as the medium reaches the glossy stage.

[six] When the image is cool, trim the excess paper, leaving a small margin around the holder. Soak the label holder pendant in water for 20 minutes.

[seven] Once the label holder pendant has been soaked, peel the paper backing from the pendant.

[eight] Do a final trim around the edges of the pendant. Try to trim a smooth edge, making sure not to expose the metal. Cut medium out of the holes in the pendant with a craft knife.

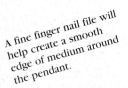

A fine finger nail file will help create a smooth edge of medium around the pendant.

tip

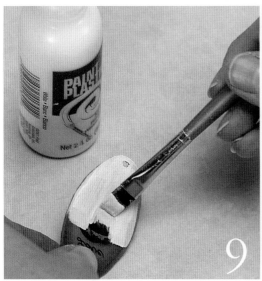

[nine] Brush one coat of white Paint for Plastic on the back of the label holder. Let the pendant dry for 48 hours. Brush on a second coat of paint and let that coat dry for another 48 hours.

[ten] Thread a plain silver washer, an oval blue bead and another washer on a head pin. Use wire cutters to cut the excess wire, leaving a ¼" (6mm) wire end. Bend the wire end into a loop using round-nose pliers.

[eleven] Cut the end off a head pin. Bend the wire end into a loop. Thread a square blue bead on the wire to the loop. Cut off the excess wire, leaving a ¼" (6mm) end. Bend that end into a loop using round-nose pliers.

[twelve] Use long-nose pliers to attach the head pin with the oval bead to the bottom hole of the label holder with a jump ring. Attach the square blue bead and the decorative silver washer to the top hole using a jump ring. Attach the barbell chain to the top loop with a jump ring.

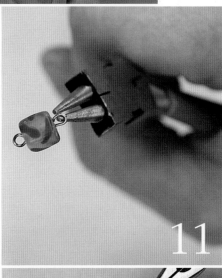

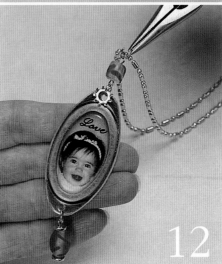

For best results, read the Transfers Unlimited instructions before starting. I've achieved greater success with a toaster oven than a conventional oven. I also highly recommend you try a few practice pieces before starting this project. **tip**

image transfer **bracelet**

What could be more fun than to make a bracelet with your children's artwork in it? This project uses a cool transfer method that embeds the images into the gold-painted label holders. This is a project guaranteed to have people asking, "How'd you do that?"

what you need

Children's art work

Transfers Unlimited kit
Artisan's Choice

Antique white square label holders
Making Memories

6mm gold jump rings

Gold toggle clasp set

Epson glossy photo paper

White Paint for Plastic
Plaid Enterprises, Inc.

18kt gold leafing pen
Krylon

Long-nose pliers

Craft knife

Scissors

Heat embossing tool

Paintbrush

Color ink-jet printer

Computer scanner

Toaster oven or oven

Aluminum foil

Paper towels

Small pan to hold water

inspiring ideas

The technique could also be used to display your children's photographs, favorite fine art pictures from postcards, or even your favorite scrapbook papers. Just be aware of copyright laws when using someone else's art.

[one] Scan the original artwork or the images you want to use for your bracelet into a computer. Reduce each image to a size that will fit into the label holder. Make a copy of each image using an ink-jet printer on photo paper.

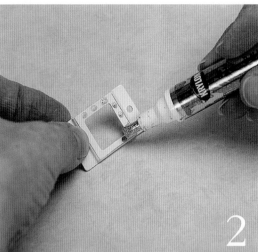

[two] Use the gold leafing pen to decorate the label holders as desired. Let the decorations dry overnight before continuing.

[three] Make a liquid transfer of the color images with the label holders using the Transfers Unlimited kit. See pages 63-64 for more detailed instructions on these procedures. Remove the paper backing, trim away the excess medium and cut away the medium from the holes using a fresh blade in a craft knife. Paint the back with white paint and let it dry for 48 hours. If necessary, apply a second coat.

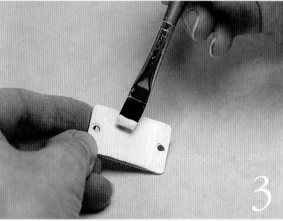

[four] Connect the label holders together with jump rings, using long-nose pliers. Add a clasp set with jump rings.

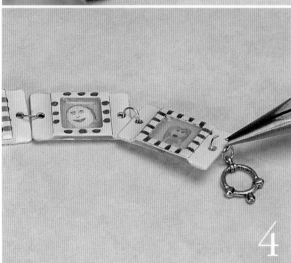

Before starting, practice the transfer method on extra color copies. And for best results on the bracelet, transfer just one image at a time.

tip

photo charm **bracelet**

Making a charm bracelet with large, colorful foil beads is a good way to update this form of jewelry. Copper, silver and gold mini hang tags add another modern element. Personalize the artwork with your favorite photos, or give the bracelet as a memento gift with photos from a special event such as a wedding or anniversary.

what you need

Favorite photographs

Mini hang tags in assorted shapes and metal colors

Glass foil beads mix

4mm x 5mm silver and gold metal rondelle beads

2mm crimp beads

Assorted jump rings in gold or silver

Spring ring clasp set

Thin beading cord

Craft glue

Dimensional glaze

Masking tape (optional)

Long-nose pliers

Wire cutters

Scissors

Small flat brush

Color copier

Ruler

Sheet of paper (optional)

inspiring **ideas**

The mini hang tags used in this project could also be filled with scrapbook papers, writing or a sequence of pictures for a completely different type of bracelet. The procedure used on photo images would be the same for scrapbook papers.

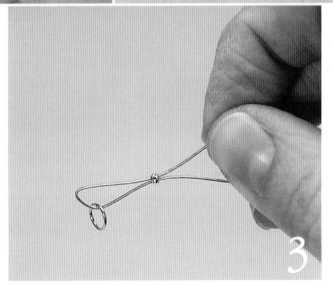

[one] Make color copies of selected photos, reducing them so they are small enough to fit in the hang tags. Cut out the images for the tags using the paper templates provided with the hang tags.

[two] Insert the images into the hang tag frames, gluing them in place. Let them dry thoroughly. Brush the photo images in the tags with two coats of dimensional glaze, allowing adequate drying time between coats.

[three] Cut a 10" (25cm) piece of beading cord. Thread one crimp bead and a jump ring on the end of the cord. Loop the end of the cord back through the crimp bead.

tip

To keep the charms from moving when you brush on the dimensional glaze, roll up small pieces of masking tape and tape the tags to a piece of scrap paper.

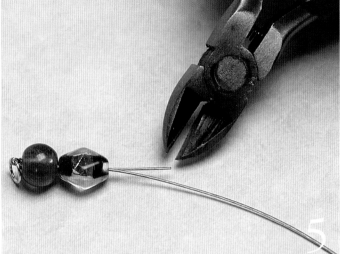

[**four**] Slide the crimp bead to the jump ring. Flatten the crimp bead down over the two strands of cord using long-nose pliers. Make sure the crimp bead is crushed and cannot slip off the cord.

[**five**] Thread two glass foil beads onto the two strands of cord. Trim excess cord from the shorter end of the cord.

[**six**] Continue threading glass foil beads and metal rondelle beads as desired (see Tip below).

[**seven**] When all beading is finished, thread one crimp bead on the end of the cord. Thread a jump ring on the cord and loop the cord end back through the crimp bead, then thread the cord end back through the last two glass foil or metal rondelle beads.

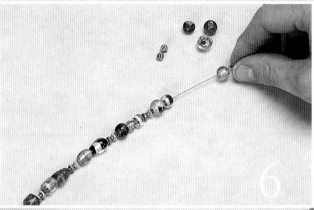

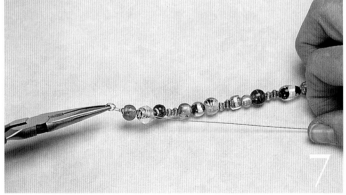

tip

If you know where you want the charms placed on the bracelet, string them on as you add the beads. I threaded two metal rondelle beads for each charm I was going to use. The rondelle beads were threaded between groups of glass foil beads approximately 1" (3cm) long.

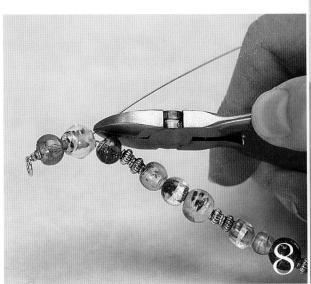

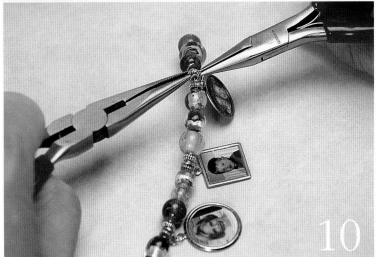

[eight] Firmly pull the cord end to close the loop. The beads should be tight on the cord, but not so close that there is no room for the jump rings connecting the photo charms. Flatten the crimp bead over the cord, making sure the crimp bead keeps the beads secure. Cut off the excess end of the cord.

[nine] Add the spring ring clasp set to the jump rings at both ends of the bracelet.

[ten] Attach the hang tag charms to the charm bracelet with jump rings, using needle-nose pliers. I used larger jump rings (6mm) between the metal rondelle beads and two small jump rings (4mm) to hang the tags from the larger jump rings.

If you're worried about the beading cord coming loose, add a second crimp bead to either side of the bracelet.

tip

beaded **barrette**

This project provides a great way to use some of the fun, nostalgic printed paper available today. A scrapbook tin tile makes a great base for the barrette and goes nicely with the accent of silver wire and beads.

what you need

Rectangular stitch tin tile
Making Memories

Finders Keepers collection collage papers
DMD

Blue Japanese glass square beads

Barrette clasp

24-gauge silver wire

Craft glue

Embellishment glue

Dimensional glaze

Long-nose pliers

Round-nose pliers

Scissors

Wire cutters

Paintbrush

Ruler

inspiring **ideas**

Since several tiles come in each pack, why not use left-overs to make matching earrings or a pin? You could also make an accent for your purse or belt by hanging the decorated tin tile from a jump ring and a small piece of bead chain.

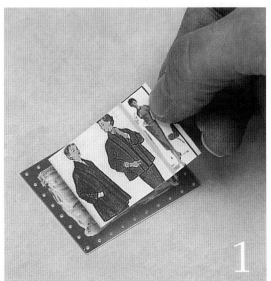

[one] Select a section of the collage papers for the barrette. From that section, cut a rectangle 1⅝" x 1¼"" (4cm x 3cm). Brush three coats of dimensional glaze on the collage paper, allowing drying time between each coat. Glue the collage paper to the tin tile using craft glue. Let dry.

[two] Cut a piece of wire 20" (41cm) long. Tightly coil 1" (3cm) at one end of the wire using round-nose pliers. Insert the other end down into the bottom left corner hole in the tin tile. Come up through the hole to the right of the coil and thread one blue bead on the wire. Insert the wire into the hole just above the coil and pull taut. Come up through the third hole on the left edge and then down through the third hole on the bottom edge, creating diagonal lines with the wire. Make two more diagonal rows of wire, threading a bead on both the third and fourth row.

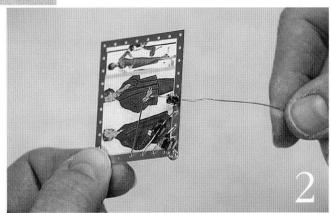

[three] Create stitches along the bottom edge with the wire, threading it up through one hole and down through the next. Make three stitches up the right edge of the pin, ending on the back of the tile. Thread the wire up through the third hole from the corner on the top edge, then come down through the third hole from the corner on the right edge. (This is the second wire to pass through this hole; use an awl to enlarge the hole if needed). Thread the wire up through the second hole on the right side, thread a bead on the wire, and then go down through the second hole on the top. Thread the wire through the hole in the upper right corner. Trim the wire to leave 1" (3cm) and coil the end tightly with the round-nose pliers.

[four] Cut a new wire 10" (25cm) long and secure it to the back of the tile by wrapping the end around a stitch on the left edge. Insert the wire up through the hole where the fourth diagonal stitch ends and make stitches up the left side and across the top until you reach the diagonal line at the top right corner.

[five] Wrap the remaining wire around an existing wire on the back, and then cut the excess. Adhere the barrette clasp to the tin tile back using adhesive. You can use your hands to gently bend the curve in the barrette clasp a little flatter to rest against the tin tile. Let the adhesive dry before using.

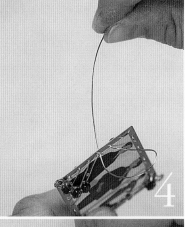

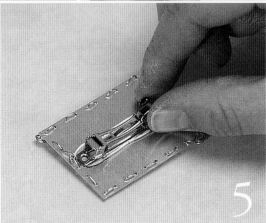

keepsake **pendant**

Transfer jewelry is an innovative new way to display your favorite keepsake picture and preserve memories safely. The colorful image and a decorated keepsake frame accented with glass beads is a winning combination.

what you need

Color photo of your choice

Color ink-jet transparency film *Grafix*

I kan'dee keepsake frame *Pebbles, Inc.*

Glass and wire beads mix

6mm silver jump rings

Silver hook-and-eye clasp

20-gauge silver wire

Delta Ceramcoat acrylic paints: Jubilee Green, Black, Opaque Red and Navy Blue *Delta Technical Coatings*

Varnish

Metal primer

Embellishment glue

Long-nose pliers

Scissors

Rond-nose pliers

Wire cutters

Fine paintbrush

Fine sandpaper

Color ink-jet copier

Pencil

Ruler

Toothpick

White paper

inspiring **ideas**

A pendant like this doesn't need to be strung on a beaded chain. Try hanging it from decorative eyelash yarn, a pretty ribbon or a silver ball chain.

74

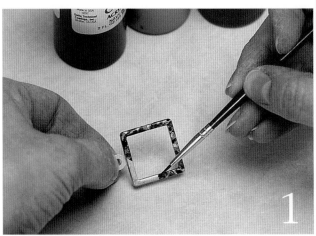

[**one**] Sand the surface of the keepsake frame and circular frame back, then apply metal primer. Let dry. Apply various colors of acrylic paints to the frame and circular back, letting the colors blend. When all the layers are dry, apply two coats of varnish, allowing drying time between coats.

[**two**] Trace the inside circle area of the frame back in the center of a piece of white paper. Cut the circle shape out of the white paper.

[**three**] Use the piece of paper with the circular hole you just made to choose the area of a photo to feature in the transparency pendant.

[**four**] Place the white paper on the photo so the image you've chosen appears in the hole in the paper. Copy the image onto the color ink-jet transparency film using a color ink-jet copier.

Try to choose paint colors for the frame that pick up colors in the beads.

tip

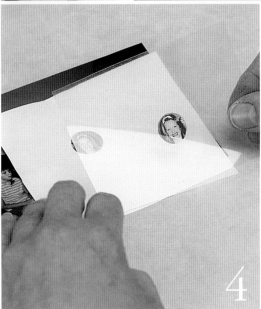

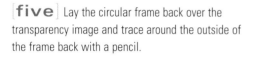

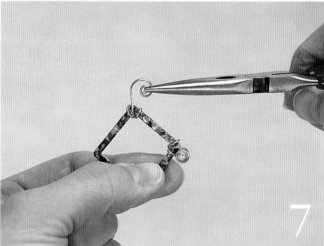

[**five**] Lay the circular frame back over the transparency image and trace around the outside of the frame back with a pencil.

[**six**] Cut out the transparency image inside the pencil line you just made. Trim the acrylic film that came with the frame into the same size circle.

[**seven**] Cut four pieces of silver wire, each 4" (10cm) long. Wrap one end of the wire over the corner of the frame two or three times, making sure the wire end is secure and hidden inside the frame. Coil the other end of the wire outside the frame corner. Trim any excess wire. Do this for each corner of the frame.

[**eight**] Insert the acrylic film, the color transparency image (with the ink surface forward) and the circular frame back into the larger frame.

[**nine**] Apply embellishment glue with a toothpick to the frame back where it connects to the larger frame. Let it dry.

[**ten**] Connect fancy wire beads together with jump rings, using long-nose pliers. Add a hook-and-eye clasp to the bead necklace using jump rings.

[**eleven**] Connect a jump ring to the frame, then connect that jump ring to the jump ring in the center of the beaded necklace.

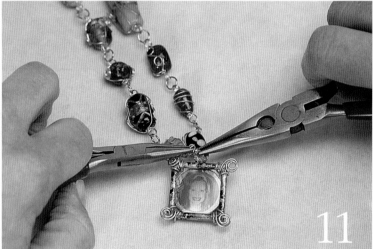

When selecting a photo for this transfer method, be sure to use a highly colorful one so the transferred image doesn't look too washed out.

tip

resources

7gypsies
(800) 588-6707
www.sevengypsies.com
In/Out Spirales pg. 26; Paris Librarie
Layers transparencies pg. 54; tiny gold
tassels pg. 60

American Crafts
(800) 879-5785
www.americancrafts.com
Slick Writer black ink pen pg. 62

American Tag
(800) 223-3956
www.americantag.net
nickel ball and chain pg. 42;
nickel barbell chain pg. 62

**American
Traditional Designs**
(800) 448-6656
www.americantraditional.com
Lil' Clips silver star clip #LC-0016 pg. 28;
Bits of Time transfers #RO-1022 pg. 46;
Lil' Clips cherish clip pg. 34

ARTchix Studio
(250) 370-9985
www.artchixstudio.com
Silver round frame bracelet pg. 16; drop
pendants pg. 26; green, red and purple
bottle caps pg. 42; metal type paper images
pg. 42; brass hinge-top frame necklace pg.
54; brass French Eiffel Tower charm pg. 54

Artisan's Choice
(877) 727-8472
www.artisanschoice.com
Transfers Unlimited kit pg. 62, 66

Beacon Adhesives
(914) 699-3400
www.beaconcreates.com
Quik Grip all purpose permanent adhesive
pg. 20, 26, 32, 60; Glass, Metal & More
permanent glue pg. 28, 74

Blue Moon Beads
(800) 377-6715
www.bluemoonbeads.com
Gold ear wires pg. 18; glass goldstone
beads #59135 pg. 20; gold bead tube
#55255 pg. 20; gold rondelle bead #55275
pg. 20, 22; gold love charms #48564 pg. 20;
silver toggle clasp #55465 pg. 24; Czech
glass green teardrop beads pg. 26; gold
clamshell earring findings pg. 26; Japanese
gold square beads #58575 pg. 28; silver star
beads #52885 pg. 28, 30; glass foil mix
beads #59125 pg. 68; gold rochaille beads
pg. 68; 7" gold charm bracelet pg. 40; gold
metal beads #53015 pg. 40; Japanese green
square beads #58625 pg. 40; create charm
pg. 42; glass matte ocean mix pg. 62; 4mm
x 5mm silver and gold metal rondelle beads
pg 68; Japanese blue square beads #58675
pg. 72; glass and wire beads mix #59115
pg. 74; silver hook and eye clasp #43384
pg. 74

Colorbök
www.colorbok.com
My Type concho brad alphabet pieces pg. 24

Crafts, Etc!
(800) 888-0321
www.craftsetc.com
gold corrugate ring spacers and red confetti
beads pg. 22; gold jewelry bells pg. 32

Daisy D's
(888) 601-8955
www.daisydspaper.com
Rectangle frame charm #7093 pg. 60

**Delta Technical
Coatings, Inc.**
(800) 423-4135
www.deltacrafts.com
Delta Ceramcoat metal primer pg. 26, 34,
50, 74; Delta Ceramcoat gloss exterior/inte-
rior varnish pg. 26, 34, 50, 74; Delta
Ceramcoat acrylic paints pg. 34, 50, 74

Deluxe Designs
(480) 497-9005
www.deluxecuts.com
Laser cut tag #32-009 pg. 38

Duncan Enterprises
(800) 438-6226
www.duncancrafts.com
Aleene's Glass & Bead Slick Surfaces
adhesive pg. 16, 46, 72; Aleene's 2 in 1 glue
pg. 38; Aleene's Paper Glaze pg. 38, 42, 46,
50, 68, 72; Aleene's Fast Grab Tacky Glue
pg. 42, 46, 50, 68, 72

EK Success Ltd.
(800) 524-1349
www.eksuccess.com
T-pin #RSNA009 pg. 20; The Attic Collection
paper clips pg. 32; The Attic Collection
small washers pg. 32; Meadow Green paper
#EKBPC106 pg. 40; Nostalgiques Botanical
epoxy donuts pg. 48

Grafix
(800) 447-2349
www.grafixarts.com
Ink-jet transparency film pg. 74

Halcraft USA
(212) 376-1580
www.halcraft.com
Red marbles mix pg. 16, gold marbles pg. 60

Heirlooms By Design
(515) 274-3602
www.heirloomsbydesign.com

**Hirschberg Schultz
& Co., Inc.**
(800) 221-8640
Gold and silver spacers pg. 50

**Jest Charming
Embellishments**
(702) 564-5101
www.jestcharming.com
Gold decorative washers pg.18, 26;
Silver decorative washers pg. 62

KI Memories, Inc.
(972) 243-5595
www.kimemories.com
Red Hot Flowers: Icicles #842 pg. 22

Krylon Products Group
(800) 457-9566
www.krylon.com
18kt Gold Leafing pen pg. 40, 66

Magic Scraps
(972) 238-1838
www.magicscraps.com
Nickel square conchos pg. 30

Making Memories
(800) 286-5263
www.makingmemories.com
Triangle paper clips pg. 26; oval label
holders pg. 62; square label holders pg. 66;
stitched tin tiles pg. 72

Memory Bound, Inc.
(515) 965-1102
www.scrappershaven.com

NRN Designs
www.nrndesigns.com
Seaside collage paper #B12281 pg. 38

Nunn Design
(360) 379-3557
Mini hang tags pg. 18, 46, 68; copper ribbon
slides pg. 18; gold star pg. 28; fleur charm
pg. 46; silver ribbon slides pg. 30; gold and
silver decorative links pg. 50

Quill Lincolnshire, Inc.
(800) 789-1331
www.quillcorp.com
Gold washers pg. 32, 48

Pebbles, Inc.
(801) 235-1520
www.pebblesinc.com
Nature cardstock stickers #36201 pg. 40;
I kan'dee keepsake frame pg. 74

Plaid Enterprises, Inc.
(800) 842-4197
www.plaidonline.com
White plastic paint pg. 62, 66

**Rupert, Gibbon
& Spider, Inc.**
(800) 442-0455
www.jacquardproducts.com
Jacquard Pearl Ex Duo Blue-Green pigment
pg. 26; Jacquard Pearl Ex pigments pg. 34

Westrim Crafts
(800) 727-2727
www.westrimcrafts.com
silver jump rings pg. 16, 24, 28, 42 62, 68,
74; gold jump rings pg. 18, 26, 32, 38, 40,
54, 60, 66; 68, red rochaille beads pg. 20;
gold head pins pg. 20, 22, 28, 38, 40; gold
beads pg. 22, 28; gold post w/ball & drop
earring findings pg. 22, 38; gold spacers pg.
22, 54; silver toggle clasp set pg. 24, silver
eye pins pg. 28; gold pin back pg. 28, 32, 60;
silver key chain split ring pg. 34; silver lanyard hook pg. 34; gold ear nuts pg. 38; gold
spring ring clasp set pg. 38, 50, 54, 68; silver beads pg. 42; silver washers pg. 42, 62;
silver head pins pg. 42, 62; butterfly clutch
& tie tac set pg. 46; gold earwire findings
pg. 48; gold toggle clasp set pg. 66; barrette
clasp pg. 72

index

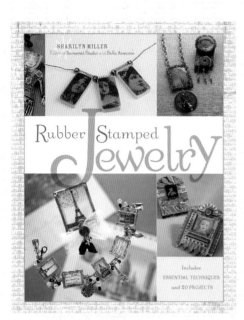

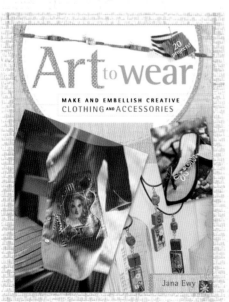

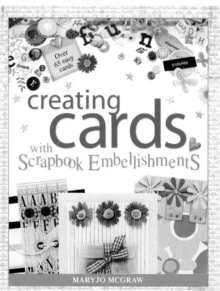